·Brothers & Sisters·

·Brothers & Sisters·

by Ellen B. Senisi

Cartwheel BOOKS™

SCHOLASTIC INC.

New York Toronto London Auckland Sydney

To John and to all fathers
who share housework and child care
so their partners can fulfill their goals.
—E. S.

Copyright © 1993 by Ellen B. Senisi.
All rights reserved. Published by Scholastic Inc.
CARTWHEEL BOOKS is a trademark of Scholastic Inc.

No part of this publication may be reproduced in whole or in part,
or stored in a retrieval system, or transmitted in any form or by any means,
electronic, mechanical, photocopying, recording, or otherwise,
without written permission of the publisher.
For information regarding permission, write to Scholastic Inc.,
730 Broadway, New York, NY 10003.

Library of Congress Cataloging-in-Publication Data

Senisi, Ellen B.
Brothers & sisters / by Ellen B. Senisi
p.   cm.
ISBN 0-590-46419-1
1. Brothers and sisters—Juvenile literature.   I. Title.   II. Title: Brothers and sisters.
BF723.S43S35   1993
306.875'3—dc20   92-42912   CIP   AC

12 11 10 9 8 7 6 5 4 3 2 1   3 4 5 6 7 8/9

Printed in Singapore

First Scholastic printing, September 1993

What is it like to have a new brother or sister? Tori is going to find out soon. Her mother is going to have a baby. "Is it going to be a boy or a girl?" Tori wonders. "Will Mommy love me as much when the baby comes?"

Ben has a newborn brother, and Dorrie has a new sister. Sometimes having a baby in the family is fun.

"Our new baby is so soft and tiny that I want to cuddle her all the time," says Dorrie.

But sometimes a baby is not so much fun.

"Babies can't do anything by themselves," says Ben. "Mommy still loves me. But she is so busy taking care of the baby, I have to play by myself until he takes another nap."

"I'm so tired of hearing everyone say how cute the baby is," says Valerie.

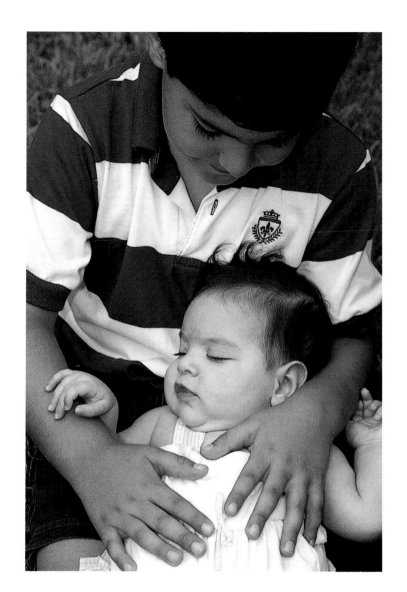 

"I like to hold my baby sister all by myself," says Michael.
So does Leo.

Jasmine and Juanita have baby sisters who have learned how to walk. "She's old enough to get into trouble now," says Jasmine, "lots of trouble."

"I help distract my sister," says Juanita. "My mom
says I'm the best helper with the baby."

"My sister always wants to do what I'm doing, but she doesn't play games the way you're supposed to," says Alicia.

"Sometimes," says Judson, "we have so much fun together."

Rena is older than her sister. "I know things my little sister doesn't," says Rena. "Now that she is in kindergarten, I can help her get ready in the morning. And I can take her to her classroom."

"You learn to share when you have a sister," Tori says.
"It's hardest to share our parents," says Rena.

Katelyn and Jordan are almost the same age. So are Ben and Suzannah.

"Sometimes, we're best friends," says Jordan.

"And sometimes we're worst enemies," says Katelyn.

Jeremy and Jonathan are twins. "We have each other to play with all the time," says Jeremy.

Ian and Ryan are twins, too. "Dad says that we even sleep the same way," says Ryan. "We like looking so much alike that we can trick people."

"We aren't exactly alike, though," says Ian. "I'm better at drawing, but my brother is better at sports."

Sometimes it's hard to be a younger brother.
"It's not fair!" says Peter. "Just because she's older, my sister can do everything better."

And sometimes it's great to be a younger brother.

"She's my other mom," says Steven.

"We have our own secrets," says Tyler.

"And we have our own special games."

Trey's older brother and Jesse's older sister are both in middle school.

"He gets mad at me because he thinks I'm a pest," says Trey.

"We get mad at each other a lot," says Jesse. "But then we forget about it."

"Sometimes, my sister is the only person who understands how I feel," says Juanita.

Alex has a teenage brother, and Bianca has a teenage sister. "When can I go everywhere and do everything, just like her?" Bianca wonders.

"Sometimes my sister acts like a grown-up, and we don't have anything to talk about," says Maura. "Other times she's just like me."

"I was adopted," says Sujathi. "Jessica and I came from different moms and dads. But we're still sisters—forever."

Laura and Emma were also adopted. "I tell everybody right away, 'This is my sister!'"

"My dad told me that when they were kids, he and my uncle got into fights. But they still liked each other the best," says Will. "They're grown-ups now and they help each other a lot. They let me help, too."

"My mom said she and her sister used to play school all the time. Now it's for real because they're both teachers," says Eddie. "My mom says her sister is more important to her than ever."

"My grandma and my great-aunt have been sisters for seventy years," says Katherine. "Grandma says her sister is *still* her best friend."